"**A**lthough some writers continue to argue that submarine *I-25* was beyond the range of the big guns of Battery Russell, and that *I-25* was under way while it was firing, and some events on the night of the attack at Fort Stevens, as portrayed by Bert Webber, are at variance with what happened, and that the phony chart in the hands of an historical society was skipper Tagami's chart, the prime factors of this incident in Oregon military history have been thoroughly documented by Bert Webber's amazing research from absolute prime sources. Let us leave the unbelievers wallow."

—Don McArthur, World War-II Japanese Military Specialist
Aberdeen, Washington
March 14, 1995

PANIC!

Fort Stevens Target of Jap Submarine's Guns

9 Shells Scream Ashore On Oregon Coast; Army Announces Damage Nil

Hear! Hear! Hear!

Victory Center, at noon Tuesday, hear the famous Bremerton Navy Yard band, and Bob Nichols' Hawaiians; see the Fighting Patters and then buy war savings bonds.

The Oregonian

VOL. LXXXI—NO. 25,477   PORTLAND, OREGON, TUESDAY, JUNE 23, 194_   CITY EDITION   24 PAGES   PRICE FIVE CENTS

Shells From Japanese Submarine Leave Scars But No Damage on Oregon Coast

BY HERMAN EDWARDS
Staff Writer, The Oregonian

(Eyewitness Account on Page 6. See Wirephoto Page. Also)

ASTORIA, June 23 (Special)—Nine high-velocity projectiles, probably fired from a five-inch rifle on the deck of a large Japanese submarine fell screaming near the Fort Stevens military reservation Sunday night, signalling Japan's first attack on a primary military objective in continental United States.

No damage was done and no persons were injured, although the hurting shells came dangerously close to their objective and one buried itself in a swamp within a scant 200 yards of a sleeping family of six persons. Others struck sand ridges, exploding harmlessly.

Many Report Attack

The attack, which began at 11:38 P. M., stirred residents of Astoria hillside residential sections and scores of persons along the popular Clatsop vacation beaches from sleep. Dozens told of hearing the roar of the submarine's gun and some said they saw the muzzle flash.

The authorities first released official word of the attack early Monday.

The shells came "too damn close," said Colonel Carl S. Doney, commanding officer of the harbor defenses of the Columbia, who permitted a mine planter and phonograph the roasting made by the exploding projectiles.

The attacking ship undoubtedly was a submarine and fired from a distance of several miles offshore, said Colonel Doney.

Big Gun Used

"Fragments taken from one of the shell craters indicated that they probably came from a five-inch gun, capable of firing 16,000 to 18,000 yards," said the colonel.

One large fragment taken from this crater while newsmen were present measured approximately seven inches in length and three-fourths of an inch in thickness. A portion of the base of the shell fragment was about 18 inches long and weighed in the neighborhood of 60 pounds.

The submarine was firing from a position approximately due west of Fort Stevens, officers said. All agreed that nine shots were fired.

One of the shells came down in swampy ground along the Delaura road, south of Fort Stevens proper and less than 200 yards from the residence of Mr. and Mrs. Gene Heffling. The Hefflings and three of their children, aged 9, 1 and 3, were awake. Many persons saw the projectile, but a 13-year-old boy slept through it without waking.

FORT STEVENS Major Fry Stewart exhibits one of the fragments of the Jap shell.

SHELL CRATER An officer (lower right) recovers a shell fragment from crater where a projectile fell in marshy ground and hands it to Colonel Carl S. Doney, commanding officer of the Harbor Defense of the Columbia.

Mid-East, South Russia

Navy Silent

PANIC!

at Fort Stevens

Japanese Navy Shells Fort Stevens, Oregon in World War-II

—Documentary—   Bert Webber

Webb Research Group Publishers
Books About the Oregon Country

Published by
WEBB RESEARCH GROUP PUBLISHERS
Books About the Oregon Country
P. O. Box 314
Medford, Oregon 97501

Photographs are from the Bert Webber collection
having accumulated over a period of about twenty years

Library of Congress Cataloging-in-Publication Data

Webber, Bert.
    Panic! at Fort Stevens : Japanese navy shells Fort Stevens,
Oregon in World War II : documentary / Bert Webber.
            p. 94.   cm.
    Includes bibliographical references and index.
    ISBN 0-936738-87-1
    1. World War, 1939-1945—Naval operations–Submarine. 2.
World War, 1939-1945–Naval operations, Japanese. 3. Fort
Stevens (Oregon) I. Title.
D783.6.W43   1995   95-14782
940.54'28—dc20   CIP

Contents

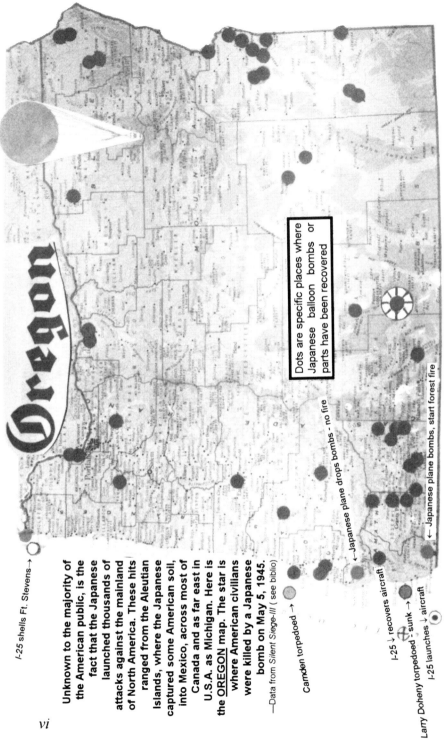

Oregon

Unknown to the majority of the American public, is the fact that the Japanese launched thousands of attacks against the mainland of North America. These hits ranged from the Aleutian Islands, where the Japanese captured some American soil, into Mexico, across most of Canada and as far east in U.S.A. as Michigan. Here is the OREGON map. The star is where American civilians were killed by a Japanese bomb on May 5, 1945.

—Data from *Silent Siege-III* (see biblio)

Dots are specific places where Japanese balloon bombs or parts have been recovered

I-25 shells Ft. Stevens →

Camden torpedoed →

← Japanese plane drops bombs - no fire

← Japanese plane bombs, start forest fire

I-25 ↓ recovers aircraft

Larry Doheny torpedoed ↓ sunk →

I-25 launches ↓ aircraft

Introduction

The Japanese Navy's attack at Fort Stevens, at the mouth of the Columbia River in Oregon, made headlines in newspapers from Oregon to New York. The initial reports were understandably sketchy then feature stories emerged over the next few days.

> There has been a long-standing need for a small book that sets forth the story of the Japanese attack at Fort Stevens Oregon. The subject makes up Chapter 6 in *Silent Siege-III, Japanese Attacks on North America in World War-II, Ships Sunk, Air raids, Bombs Dropped, Civilians Killed*. The text in the present book is based on that chapter.   —The editor

This enemy action on Home Soil-U.S.A. was not unexpected by the American military leaders, but the audacity of such an attack was the farthest thing in the minds of most civilians. It is a fact that a very large percentage of Americans had a "business-as-usual" attitude about the war. It was almost a so-so attitude when in the spring of 1942, all three of the west coast states and

---

Chronology of Japanese Attacks on the Mainland of the U.S.

December 1941. Japanese submarines damage and sink ships along the West Coast.

February 1942. Japanese Navy shells an oil field at Goleta California.

June 1942. Japanese Navy shells Fort Stevens, Oregon.

September 1942. Japanese Navy airplane bombs Siskiyou National Forest in Oregon - starts forest fire. More ships sunk.

November 1944 - spring 1945. Japanese Army bombs United States and Canada by sending stratosphere-floating balloons carrying at least 30,000 bombs. Oregon bombed 45 times - civilians killed in Oregon
                                                      —Data from *Silent Siege-III*

---

lower part of Arizona were declared "Military Areas" from which "any or all persons may be excluded."*

This public attitude changed when the government started rationing automobile tires, gasoline, shoes and even food.

---

* The quotation is from Executive Order 9066 February 19, 1942. The order did not single out Japanese, as the majority of today's politically correct commentators choose to believe. For the accurate account, refer to *American and Japanese Relocation in World War-II, Fact, Fiction & Fallacy*. The Executive Order appears on page 22. See bibliography.

The first story in the *Oregonian* about the attack at Fort Stevens (June 23) brazenly declared "**9 Shells Scream Ashore on Oregon Coast**."

Some people near the scene were asked the number they counted and many numbers popped up. If any number is to be believed, we concluded it would be in the official *Log* of the attacking Japanese vessel. "Nine" shots? The *Log* reads 17!

For decades there has been almost a conspiracy to protect the decision of the military commanders at Fort Stevens who concluded that the attacking vessel was "out of range." How would they know? It was a black night. The submarine was painted black. It didn't show any lights - just gun flashes. The one true way, at the time, was to turn on the searchlights. But the commanders refused to allow any lights be turned on. The commanders never allowed the big guns to return the fire whether they'd hit anything or not.

(Various accounts about a RADAR on Cape Disappointment have been reviewed, but, as we shall see, these reports are inconclusive.)

We asked the Japanese ship's skipper if he knew exactly where he was when his gunners started shooting. He did. When he learned he was under the noses of big coast defense guns, he was shocked declaring: "To risk my ship and my crew with such foolishness was unthinkable."

Some American writers insist that the submarine was under way (moving) during the shooting. To refute this we turn to the submarine's skipper, Commander Meiji Tagami. He said his ship was not moving, other than from the swell of the sea. This is reinforced by Admiral Hiroichi Samejima from *Senchio Sosho (Boeicho Kenshujo Senshishitsu) The Aleutian's.* (See bibliography)

All of these issues are in this present small book.

I appreciate the willing assistance of many people who worked with me over the years to make this story complete. The long list of 65 individuals appears on page 284 of *Silent Siege-III.*

Bert Webber, M.L.S.
Research Photojournalist
Central Point, Oregon
Spring 1995

Prologue to Panic

Sunday, June 21, 1942, had been a pleasant day at the mouth of the Columbia River. Weather observer Fred Andrus recorded a temperature of 72° F., clear sky, and wind from the northwest at 4 knots. Captain Jack R. Wood, 249th Coast Artillery (Harbor Defense), the commander at Battery Russell at Fort Stevens, did not leave the post even though his Battery was not on duty. But his wife had come from their apartment in nearby Warrenton for a visit.

At a resort hotel in Gearhart, 15 miles south, U.S. Supreme Court Justice William O. Douglas had addressed the Oregon Newspaper Publishers Association the night before. Most of his audience had left for home, but he had stayed to enjoy the week-end and thus was on hand to witness the unusual offshore fire-works that Sunday night.

As night came on, the air cooled but the skies stayed clear. Although there was supposed to be a dimout along the coast be-cause a submarine, with a big deck gun, had shelled the Estevan Point lighthouse on Vancouver Island the night before, lights blazed in Seaside. This was a resort town on the beach two miles south of Gearhart. Many people followed their normal patterns of activity apparently unaware that a world war had been under way for the past six months.

As reconstructed by Jack Fink, planetarium astronomer at Medford, Oregon Senior High School, sunset was at 7:54 p.m. This was the longest day of the year, and evening twilight lasted until 10:30 p.m. The moon, just past the first quarter, was due to set at 12:16 a..m. The Tongue Point Naval Air Station reported at 11:30 p.m.:

> Light clouds, less than .3 cover at 40,000 feet.
> Temperature: 57° F.
> Wind: north 3 knots.
> Barometric pressure: 30.20.

GEARHART HOTEL

All during the war, there were rumors of signaling between offshore Japanese war ships and persons, presumed to have been Japanese, on shore. If this was true early in the war and submarine *I-25* was receiving "intelligence" from shore, would it be plausible that the spy advised the sub that a Justice of the U. S. Supreme was at the Gearhart Hotel? If so, wouldn't it have been a plum in the Japanese war-making hat to have killed the jurist by shelling the hotel?

However: By late June, when this event occurred, and the judge was staying at the hotel, all Germans, Italians and Japanese had been ordered out of the coastal area of Oregon thus there were no Japanese there.

The submarine did not attack the hotel but did shoot in the direction of Fort Stevens, about ten miles north, from a position at sea. When the sub's commander was asked if he knew about the Gearhart Hotel during an interview with the author 33 years later, he said he did not know of the hotel's presence and there was no one on shore communicating with his submarine.

The hotel was demolished in 1972 to make way for condominiums.   —Bert Webber photo

At Fort Stevens, on Fire Control Hill, Major Robert Huston, Senior Duty Officer, and Corporal "Tully" were on duty.

Technical Sergeant Vernon Greig and Sergeant Gil Mather were getting ready for bed in a room of the small non-coms' barracks in a gully behind the plotting room. In "B" Battery, at the 249th headquarters on the main cantonment, Corporal Ken Evans, a battery cook, was CQ (Charge-of-Quarters).

Battery Pratt, a battery of 6-inch guns, was the "ready" battery and Lieutenant Lynn Neeley was the duty officer. Back from his visit with his wife, Captain Wood was still in uniform in his quarters under the big guns of Battery Russell.

At "White Evelyn," the south jetty outpost, men on duty always slept with their clothes on in their underground bunker to be ready at a moment's notice to strafe the beach south of the jetty if the enemy attempted a landing.

This is one of two 6-inch guns at Battery Pratt.*

Mr. and Mrs. Cliff Hitchman, who lived on a small farm close to the post, had gone to a movie in Seaside. Their daughter Ardith, 12, and her brothers, were home and had gone to bed.

Two Coast Guard vessels, the *USCGC 402* and the *Manana II,* a converted private yacht formerly owned by Aaron Frank, a Portland department store executive, were in position inside the bar at the mouth of the Columbia. They were to meet two freighters at 4:30 the next morning and escort them through the mine fields.

*Battery Pratt was the "Ready Battery" on the night of the Japanese attack. It faced the Columbia River. The shooting came from the wrong direction for this battery to have had anything to shoot at.

A feature of the "White Evelyn" outpost was the old railroad water tower that had its insides rebuilt as an observation post (OP). It was manned by elements of "B" Battery, 249th Coast Artillery (Harbor Defense). Had an enemy made a serious attack on the OP, either with a ship or an airplane, a single shot would probably have taken out the maze of field telephone wires and the tower itself.

The French 75mm Field Artillery cannon was nearby. It served primarily as a "challenge" gun, putting shots across the bows of ships that failed to provide recognition signals. Sometimes wayward skippers of fishing boats did not heed the warning and took a second shot that sometimes "accidentally" holed the boat.

One of four 12-inch mortars permanently mounted at Battery Clark, Fort Stevens. Mortars issued a high-arcing plunging shell that was intended to crash the wooden deck of an enemy ship. By the time World War-II came about, there were very few ships of wood construction. Battery Gunther, at Fort Canby, also equipped with a four mortar battery, was on the north side of the Columbia River

Across the Columbia River, the lighthouse on Cape Disappointment was sending out beams of red and white light powerful enough to be seen 21 miles at sea. At Fort Canby, Captain Zed Harris had put the 12-inch mortars of Battery Gunther to bed as his unit was not on alert that night. He had notified duty officer Neeley, at Battery Pratt, and was getting ready for sleep himself.

At nearby McKenzie Head, Richard Ebi, Private Joe Campbell, and another member of a searchlight unit were playing cards to pass the time during their all-night duty period.

George "Jud" Weber was a searchlight man and is shown with a portable 60-inch Sperry model. The "portability" was that it had wheels. But these First World War type wheels limited any other than minimal moving of the light once it was unloaded from its transport truck. Each searchlight also came with a portable generator with the same type of wheels. Earlier searchlights were only 36-inch diameter but these had been largely replaced with the larger units by the outbreak of World War-II.

A 60-inch searchlight (with post-WW-II truck wheels) is on exhibit at Fort Stevens State Park today. See page 91.

Panic — submarine!

Into this tranquil scene rose the long black hull of a submarine. The Japanese aircraft-carrier *I-25* submarine had come in through a fishing fleet because its commander, Meiji Tagami, knew there would be no mines where these boats were cruising. On the sub, the deck lookouts and the gun crews scrambled up and out of the hatch to their stations. The submarine swung around with its stern toward the shore so that the deck gun would have a clear field of fire and the submarine could leave for the open sea in a hurry if necessary.

As Sensuke Tao (formerly Sensuke Izutu) took his position as chief gunner at the brace of 25-mm machine guns, he could see the lights of a city on shore. He also noted that the preparations for the firing of the deck gun were not going smoothly. He joined Commander Tagami, Air Officer Fujita,* and the gun crew on the aft deck to give advice about adjustments and to help pass ammunition. "We elevated the gun to 30-40 degrees," Tao says. "I myself fired some shells."

Commander Tagami had the impression there was a submarine base on the Columbia River and ordered firing in that direction. Sadao Iijima, a gunnery officer, was alert for possible response by the Americans. Iijima told me:

I shot the gun with my right hand keeping the optical range-finder ready at my left hand. Should we be air attacked, then I would snap on the rangefinder and elevate the gun to attack the plane. In shooting at the land I did not use any gunsight at all. I just shot.

---

* Nubuo Fujita was the pilot assigned to fly the airplane stationed aboard *I-25*. This submarine, and its sisters, were aircraft carrying subs. The U. S. Navy, as well as the British, French and Germans, had tried for many years to develop the technique but gave up. Only the Japanese were effective in putting submarines and airplanes together in a practical and workable combination. Mr. Fujita, on another mission, a few months later, flew his airplane over Oregon, dropped bombs and started a forest fire in the Siskiyou National Forest. For all the details about the ship/plane system, and Fujita's own account of his air raid, see *Silent Siege-III, Japanese Attacks on North America in World War-II, Ships Sunk, Air raids, Bombs Dropped, Civilians Killed.- Documentary.* Refer to bibliography.

Imperial Japanese Navy Class B-1 aircraft-carrying submarines were at sea during the attack on Pearl Harbor. Immediately thereafter, nine of them took up positions along the entire west coast of the United States. Their assignment was to sink "targets of opportunity" then on Christmas Eve, 1941, present a Christmas present to the American people by shooting down all of the coastal lighthouses. At the last minute, that order was canceled. Submarine *I-25* would make three voyages to the Oregon coast inflicting damage on every trip. See *Silent Siege-III; Japanese Attacks on North America in World War-II* in bibliography.

Clifton M. Irwin, Colonel,
249th Coast Artillery, Harbor
Jack Wood, Captain, 249th Coast   Defense, Federalized Oregon
Artillery, Harbor Defense,   National Guard. Colonel Irwin
Federalized Oregon National   commanded the 249th. He pre-
Guard. Capt. Wood commanded   dicted war with Japan. His troops
Battery Russell. He was ready.   were ready.

On shore the sound of the gun brought an immediate reaction. Captain Wood, who commanded the 10-inch harbor defense Battery Russell, recalled:

When the first shot echoed across the harbor, I jumped off the cot and ran up to the command post. Battery Russell wasn't the "ready" battery; in fact, most of the men in "F" Battery had chicken pox and some were gone on pass. But when the first shot came, everyone who could, started running to their stations from their tents behind the battery. Most weren't dressed. Chris Murphy, my sergeant down in the ammunition room under the guns, was in shorts and T shirt. We looked like hell, but we were ready to shoot back in a couple of minutes.

Lights came on in the tents when the first alert sounded – then just as quickly went off again. Each tent had a Pres-To-Log-burning Sibley Stove in the center of the floor. In the darkness, artillerymen crashed into these stoves knocking some of them over while rushing out of the tents trying to get to the guns.

At the Harbor Defense Headquarters in the HECP, under old

Battery Mishler had the same size guns as Battery Russell. But Mishler's were not operable and not manned in World War-II. The Harbor Entrance Control Post (HECP) was built in the chambers under the guns. To camouflage the guns from spying airplanes, they were buried with beach sand. Today Mishler has been reclaimed and is open to visitors except the guns were long ago removed for metal salvage. (Take a flashlight.)

This picture of First Sergeant Laurence Rude, seated on the steps to his quarters at Fort Stevens, was made on August 30, 1942. Rude was a spit-and-polish, highly motivated 1st Sgt. He was the "executive" of B-Battery and saw to every detail of every-day life and duty of his men. He was tough but fair.

Battery Mishler, Major Frederick C. Dahlquist was Senior Duty Officer. Lt. Wilbur T. Cooney was the Junior Duty Officer. They were dressed in field uniforms and were in adjoining rooms in the "Duty Officers Quarters" section when they heard the first shot. Almost together they rushed into the Command Post to try to determine the source of the shot.

At the main garrison, Lawrence Rude, First Sergeant of "B" Battery, was awakened by confusion in the barracks:

I opened the door of my room and stood there in my drawers cussing at the guys to shut up. Some nut yells back that the Japs are shooting at us and then he tore out of the barracks. It was a real madhouse. The men were going in and out like a herd of elephants.

A 3/4-ton Dodge recon car was parked nearby. Somebody was grinding the starter then revving the engine, but the car did not move. The regular driver stuck his head out of an upstairs window. "You stupid SOB," he swore at the man (who turned out

Corporal Kenneth Evans, a cook in B-Battery, took his turn at being in charge of the barracks at night. This special "CQ" duty is handled by all non-commissioned officers on a regularly posted schedule. Evans had the duty the night the Japanese shot in the direction of the fort, took the telephone calls from the various outposts thus he goes down in history as an active participant.

When the 249th Coast Artillery (Harbor Defense) was Federalized in September 1940, a contract was let to construct enough barracks to house the command. The buildings were finished with camouflage paint. During peace-time summer drills, these troops lived in tents at Camp Clatsop (renamed Camp Rilea after the war) a few miles south.

One of several B-Battery machine gun nests that faced the ocean.

to be an officer) in the open-topped car, "Release the emergency brake!"

"You stupid SOB ... Release the emergency brake!"

One man ran out the barracks door into the dark and smacked his head on a parked truck. He cut his forehead a little and by the time he had regained his feet and staggered back into the building, his face was covered with blood. Rude remembered the incident vividly:

> The guys who saw him knew for sure he had been shot and that there must be Japs all over the place! The whole place jumped. It's a wonder somebody wasn't killed with all the itchy trigger fingers around.

Battery "B" was the outpost unit. It had a string of machine gun emplacements along the beach equipped with World War I .30-caliber Browning water-cooled machine guns. Cliff Moriarity was on duty in a nest near the wrecked *Peter Iredale,* a landmark on the Clatsop Beach since 1906. With one hand on his gun and the other cranking his EE-5 field telephone, he started calling "B's" Orderly Room where Ken Evan answered. Cliff yelled: "I wanna shoot. I wanna shoot. He's right out in front of me!"

Tech Sergeant Ernest Fieguth, the duty sergeant at the outpost at the base of the spit, "White Evelyn," recalled, "Hell, we couldn't give him permission [to fire]. All I could do was to keep talking to him so he wouldn't shoot. Besides, that Browning would not reach the sub anyway."

The telephone circuits from Fire Control Hill to the outposts along the beach were strung with Signal Corps W-110-B wire—

Colonel Vernon Greig, who was a Tech/Sergeant during World War-II, escorted author into the brush behind Battery Russell to show remnants of the buildings on Fire Control Hill. In picture (RIGHT PAGE) he points to corner in building where his bunk was located. This area has been recently cleaned up by Oregon State Parks.

three strands of steel and three of copper in twisted pair—but a fragment from one of the bursting shells cut a line running to three outposts.

Greig told the author:

The beach boys were out there alone. It was dark. Shells were whistling overhead. When their phone went dead they thought they'd had it. A patrol from the command post worked its way down to the dugouts to relieve tensions if for nothing else.

At outpost "White Evelyn," Bennett Loftsgaard was one of

those on duty. He recalls:

We were awakened in the underground bunker by Bud Nel screaming, "Get out of the sack, you guys. The Japs are here!" As we ran to the water tower we saw a flash of gunfire out to the sea on our left. I got upstairs [an observation position had been built inside the old railroad water tower] and swung the telescope around to the flash, read the azimuth off the dial, and had one of the men phone it to headquarters. A little later we got reports on the location of the target and began plotting its course. None of us realized exactly what was going on. We were closer to the submarine than anyone else, but we couldn't see it; yet some guy in headquarters was telling us where the Jap was and we were plotting his course. Later when I knew a bit more, I realized we were getting RADAR reports, but at that time even the word "radar" was top secret.

23

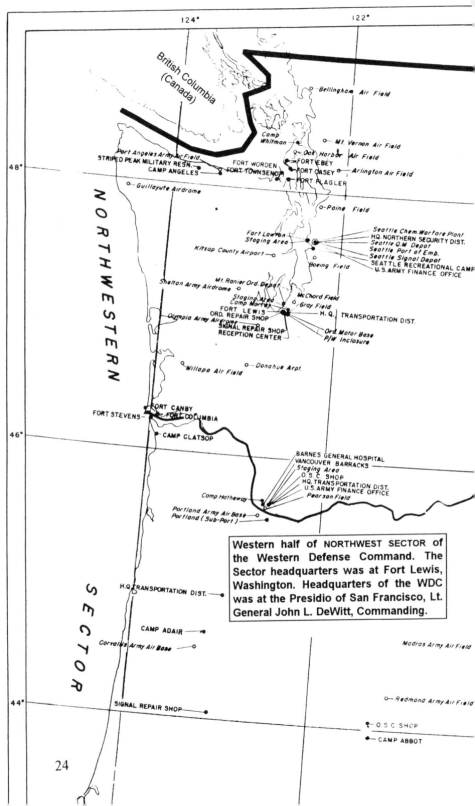

Western half of NORTHWEST SECTOR of the Western Defense Command. The Sector headquarters was at Fort Lewis, Washington. Headquarters of the WDC was at the Presidio of San Francisco, Lt. General John L. DeWitt, Commanding.

24

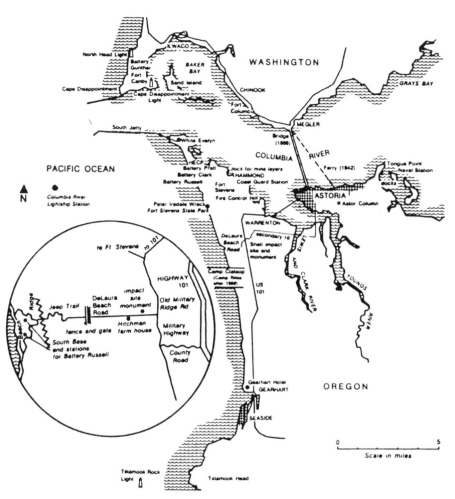

Mouth of Columbia River and vicinity.

On the Columbia River side of Fort Stevens at the Mine Battery, Sergeant Paul G. Williamson was Sergeant-of-the-Guard. He wrote:

We had just posted the guard at the boathouse, powder room and mine dock and another guard on the narrow gauge railroad which we used to transfer mine equipment to and from the dock and store room. Things had settled down when all of a sudden I hear this awful pounding on the door of the storeroom. Sergeant James L. Patterson was there and just about everyone in the platoon was screaming, 'The Japs are here! The slant-eyes are here!'

I jumped off my bunk gun in hand, and being dark I ran into the wall and scareder than hell nearly killed myself. I ran outside with cocked rifle shouting, 'Where the hell are they?' Everybody laughed yelling back, '... on the

Movement chart of 1st Submarine Flotilla (May 19, 1942 ~ July 11, 1942)

第 一 潜 水 戦 隊 行 動 図 (昭和十七年五月十九日～七月十一日)

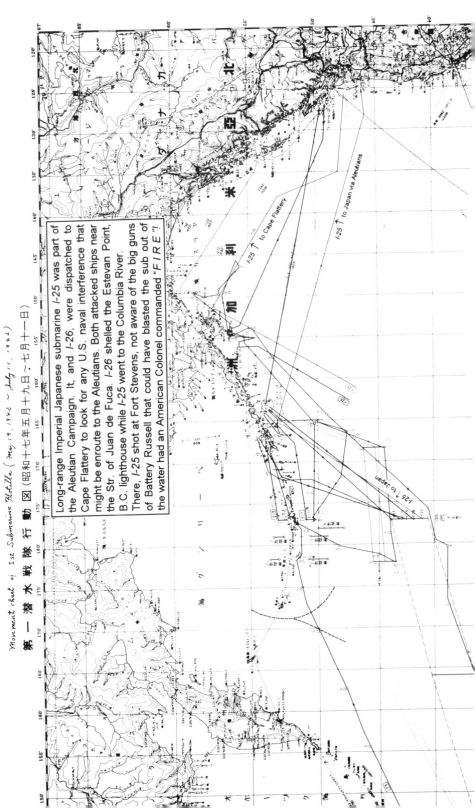

Long-range Imperial Japanese submarine *I-25* was part of the Aleutian Campaign. It, and *I-26*, were dispatched to Cape Flattery to look for any U.S. naval interference that might be enroute to the Aleutians. Both attacked ships near the Str. of Juan de Fuca. *I-26* shelled the Estevan Point, B.C. lighthouse while *I-25* went to the Columbia River. There, *I-25* shot at Fort Stevens, not aware of the big guns of Battery Russell that could have blasted the sub out of the water had an American Colonel commanded "*F I R E*".

I-25 ↑ to Cape Flattery

I-25 ↑ to Japan via Aleutians

I-25 ↓ to Japan

submarine!' Of course our location was no where near the action off Battery Russell. We were on the opposite side of the fort. Anyway, we doubled our guard from that night on until further orders.

On the north side of the river, Captain Zed Harris, commander of Battery Gunther (12-inch mortars), had just tucked himself into bed when he heard a shot which was followed by others. He sat up, kept very still not believing his ears, then recalled:

About the fourth shot, the siren at Fort Canby went off. I thought Battery Pratt [the 'ready battery'] was firing at something in the harbor. I dressed and rushed to the Battery Command Post. I saw flashes out to sea; it wasn't Pratt doing the shooting after all.

In the meantime, a score of mortar men had rushed to their positions at Gunther and were getting ready to shoot. Henry K. Scott, who was 1st Sergeant of Harris' Battery, roared into his duty station half dressed. He remembered:

Although the flashes of the Japanese gun were visible, the submarine was completely out of range and off the edge of our plotting board. Captain Harris was deeply concerned that no return fire had been opened. Finally unable to contain himself, he turned to me and asked, "Sergeant, if I made sure all phones were open, then lit a piece of paper and yelled Fire! would I be court-martialed if my guns went into action?" I could only reply, 'Yes sir'!

Harris recalls there was an Air Force RADAR on North Head which had plotted a "pip" close to the south jetty. The RADAR followed the contact as the submarine moved ever so slowly to the north, then abruptly the sub headed seaward past the blacked-out Columbia River Lightship then disappeared from the screen. (This activity at sea was after the shelling was over.)

There had been no order from the HECP or from the Columbia River Defense Command Post to turn on any searchlights. Harris contends:

I would like to have dropped mortar shells down his hatch. If we just had visibility but it was too dark. The RADAR operator had only a 1,000-yard-square grid system to work with—not accurate enough for big guns or mortars.

OFFICIAL U.S.ARMY
PHOTOGRAPHER

Firing practice at Battery Clark, Fort Stevens. The 12-inch mortars fired a high-angle plunging shell that was intended to crash on the decks of ships. The pole at left mounts a speaker for the public address system. In foreground is Sergeant Ken Moore, Official Signal Corps Cameraman from Los Angeles. He is using a Crown tripod on which is mounted a 4x5-inch Speed Graphic camera.

28

French 75mm (3-inch) Howitzer used as a "Challenge" gun at the mouth of the Columbia River. Should an incoming vessel not signal a recognition code, the ship was "challenged" to identify itself by a shot cross its bow from this gun.

According to Col. Julien Falleur of the Corps of Engineers, "Even members of the Service Command Unit manned a battery of mortars (Battery Clark) during the attack. These troops were on station and awaited the command [to fire] that night."

29

Seaside, Oregon.
Seaside has been a delightful beach-side resort com-
munity since about 1870 but it never had a housing
shortage until Worldf War II. This happned when camp
followers and army wives came to town. With Camp
Clatsop nearby, weekends were lively enough to have
Military Police roaming the streets and a Medical Detach-
ment "Pro-Station," with its green lantern at the door, on
the north edge of town. Picture post card view is typical
of late 1930's.

9 Shells Scream Ashore On Oregon Coast; Army Announces Damage Nil

BY HERMAN EDWARDS
Staff Writer, The Oregonian

(Eyewitness Account on Page 6; See Wirephoto Page, Also)

ASTORIA, June 23 (Special)—Nine high-velocity projectiles, probably fired from a five-inch rifle on the deck of a large Japanese submarine, fell screaming near the Fort Stevens military reservation Sunday night, signalling Japan's first attack on a primary military objective in continental United States.

No damage was done and no persons were injured, although the hurtling shells came dangerously close to their objective and one buried itself in a swamp within a scant 200 yards of a sleeping family of six persons. Others struck sand ridges, exploding harmlessly.

Many Report Attack

The attack, which began at 11:30 P. M., stirred residents of Astoria hillside residential sections and scores of persons along the popular Clatsop vacation beaches from sleep. Dozens told of hearing the roar of the submarine's gun and some said they saw the muzzle flash.

Army authorities first released official word of the attack early Monday.

The shells came "too damn close," said Colonel Carl S. Doney, commanding officer of the harbor defenses of the Columbia, who permitted newsmen to visit and photograph the craters made by the exploding projectiles.

The attacking ship undoubtedly was a submarine and fired from a distance of several miles offshore, said Colonel Doney.

Big Gun Used

"Fragments taken from one of the shell craters indicated that they probably came from a five-inch gun, capable of firing 16,000 to 18,000 yards," said the colonel.

One large fragment taken from this crater while newsmen were present measured approximately seven inches in length and three-fourths-inch in thickness. It indicated, said artillery officers, that the original projectile was about 16 inches long and weighed in the neighborhood of 60 pounds.

—From Oregonian June 23, 1942, Page 1

The long, wide beach (OPPOSITE PAGE) in front of Fort Stevens is the site where, in 1906, the bark *Peter Iredale* grounded. Our picture was made in 1972 when a sizable section of the bark was still standing. But it diminishes with every winter storm. During the war, the *Iredale* was the frequent target for gunnery. The main gate (THIS PAGE) as it was in 1939. The railroad, at right, brought in freight and troops from Portland.

33

Chief Petty Officer Kou Maki was SONAR operator on *I-25* and a sketch artist. He made many drawings of *I-25's* actions off the West Coast of the United States. Here (OPPOSITE PAGE) is his sketch of *I-25* shooting in the direction of a "submarine pen" when the sub was actually under the big guns of Fort Stevens. His drawing, utilizing "artist's license" shows the gun firing off the port side of the submarine. (The firing was off the stern.) There is some belief that this drawing, showing the sub under way while firing, may have added to the confusion of those who declare the vessel was moving while the attack was in process. The sketch has been used in Webber books several times. (Of course it was a pitch-black night and no one on shore actually saw the vessel.) However, it is known, from ship's log, that the submarine was not moving and merely "riding the waves" while shooting.

Custom-made replica of Japanese 5.5 cm. shell (THIS PAGE) of the type fired by *I-25* at Fort Stevens on June 21, 1942. Facsimile was built by Donald D. McArthur, Japanese Military Specialist, Aberdeen, Wash.

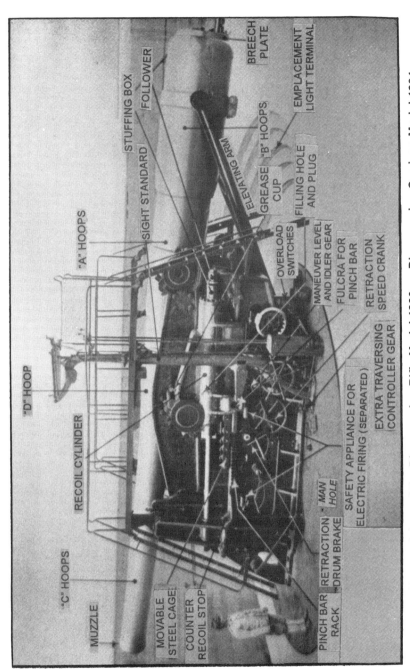

Nomenclature of the Disappearing Rifle Model 1900 on Disappearing Carriage Model 1901. Gun shown in *From Battery* (down) position.

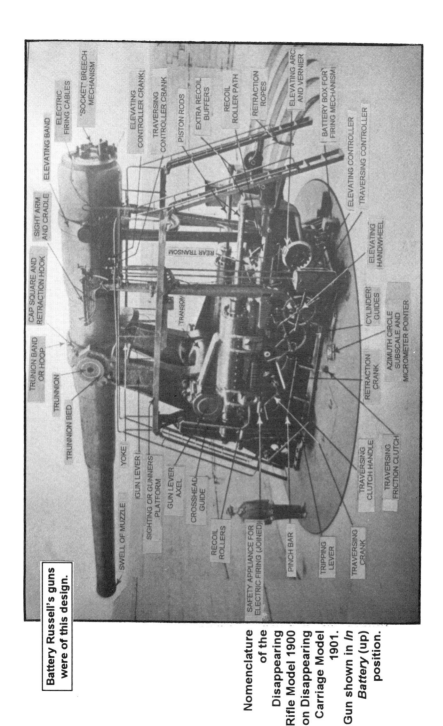

Battery Russell's guns were of this design.

Nomenclature of the Disappearing Rifle Model 1900 on Disappearing Carriage Model 1901. Gun shown in *In Battery* (up) position.

SWELL OF MUZZLE

ELEVATING BAND

ELECTRIC FIRING CABLES

SOCKET BREECH MECHANISM

TRUNNION BAND OR HOOP

TRUNNION

TRUNNION BED

CAP SQUARE AND RETRACTION HOOK

SIGHT ARM AND CRADLE

ELEVATING CONTROLLER CRANK

TRAVERSING CONTROLLER CRANK

PISTON RODS

EXTRA RECOIL BUFFERS

RECOIL ROLLER PATH

RETRACTION ROPES

ELEVATING ARC AND VERNIER

BATTERY BOX FOR FIRING MECHANISM

YOKE

GUN LEVER

SIGHTING OR GUNNERS PLATFORM

GUN LEVER AXEL

CROSSHEAD GUIDE

REAR TRANSOM

TRANSOM

ELEVATING CONTROLLER

TRAVERSING CONTROLLER

ELEVATING HANDWHEEL

CYLINDER GUIDES

RECOIL ROLLERS

SAFETY APPLIANCE FOR ELECTRIC FIRING (JOINED)

PINCH BAR

TRIPPING LEVER

TRAVERSING CRANK

TRAVERSING CLUTCH HANDLE

TRAVERSING FRICTION CLUTCH

RETRACTION CRANK

AZIMUTH CIRCLE SUBSCALE AND MICROMETER POINTER

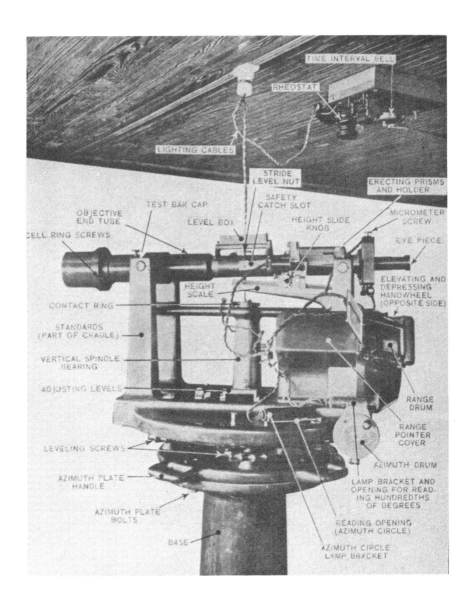

Warner and Swasey Depression Position Finder (DPF) for use with Coast Artillery.

38

One of many DPF units installed at Fort Stevens. This one was at Battery Russell. See nomenclature on page 38.

Battery F, 249th CAC (HD) men from Marshfield (renamed Coos Bay) during target practice (TOP) from Battery Russell. View from tug boat towing a target (LOWER) several miles at sea. The final objective of target practice is to develop ability to score a hit. Camera records a direct hit fired from Battery Russell. Artillerymen of the 249th Coast Artillery believed in the old saw, "Practice makes perfect." They knew their guns. They regularly shattered the targets with direct hits. The 249th, insofar as study and drill could make it, was a battle-ready unit. But when the time came to shoot at an enemy, the order *F I R E !* never came.

249TH C. A.
FT. STEVENS ORE.
MAY 8 1941
BTY. RUSSELL
FIRED BY F
SHOT NO. 9
TOW LINE 600
BATTERY ⟶

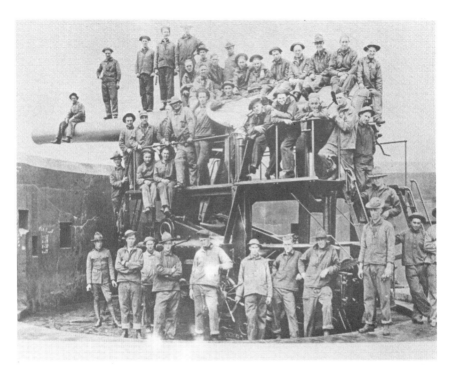

Annual summer National Guard training was held at the various guns of Fort Stevens. Incomplete records reveal this battery of men (TOP) was either 1920 or 1921. When this picture was made at a 10-inch Battery Russell gun, the men who manned this rifle in World War II were just barely being born. Battery Pratt (6-inch gun) (LOWER) staffed by the 3rd Coast Artillery in 1938.

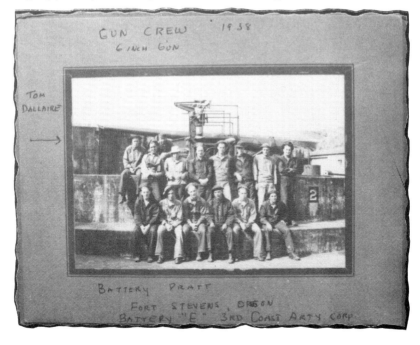

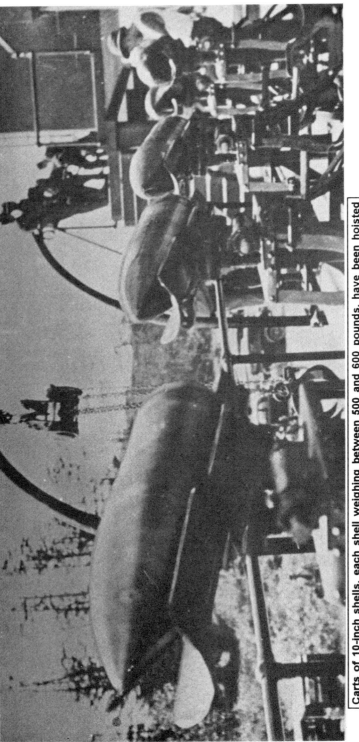

Carts of 10-inch shells, each shell weighing between 500 and 600 pounds, have been hoisted from the storage rooms under the battery to transport carts. Men pushed the steel-wheeled cart to the breech of a gun where the shell was pushed into the gun with a ram-rod (see page 44). The ever watchword was "Don't drop one on your toe."

Open breech (top) of a 10-inch gun at Battery Russell. This 10-inch shell (lower) was permanently mounted at the entrance door of the National Guard Armory in Ashland for decades. The armory was eventually declared surplus but those asked didn't know what happened to this shell.

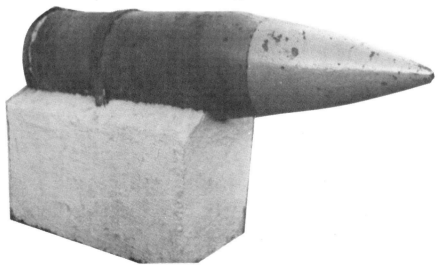

Loading a gun at Battery Russell during National Guard summer drill. Note old buildings just beyond the parapet. These were original living quarters for Point Adams Lighthouse. The lighthouse was discontinued in 1899 and dismantled in 1912. The other buildings came down in the 1930's. The unique details of the lighthouse are in *Oregon's Seacoast Lighthouses*.

—(See bibliography)

44

READY?

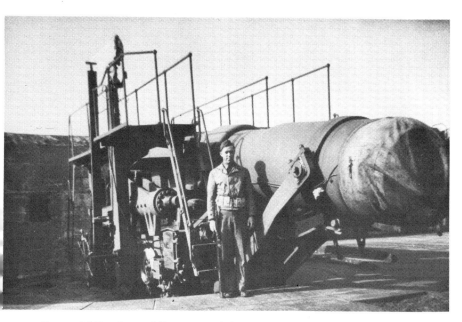

On a quiet Sunday, soldier on guard duty takes a breather to have the Inspecting Officer make a snapshot of him to send home. Then turn-about, the soldier photographs the officer for the same purpose. Generally, these civilian soldiers of the National Guard were friendly at home as well as when on duty. But there were notable exceptions.

Captain Jack Wood, 249th Coast Artillery (Harbor Defense), commanded the men who manned Battery Russell. Captain Wood knew his business and was respected by his troops.

Turn Off The Damn Light!

In the thick of the excitement, two separate orders reached the Coast Guard duty officer at the Cape Disappointment Lighthouse almost one on top of the other. Harris' report first:

> On each rotation the beam of the lighthouse was splashing across the face of the command post. I called the chief of the Coast Guard and told him to turn off the light – quick – we were being fired on. He argued. He said he didn't have authority to turn off a lighthouse in the middle of the night.

When I asked the Coast Guard District Headquarters in Seattle to search their records for happenings on that night, the then Public Information Officer Lt. Thomas Barrett wrote:

> According to the Cape Disappointment Log, at 12:35 a. m., June 22, 1942, the CO of the light station received a call from Base Astoria to extinguish Cape Disappointment and North Head lights and the Columbia River entrance range lights. He complied and these lights were extinguished at 12:46 a.m.

That was: "12:35" – order received.
That was: "12:46" – compliance.
Eleven minutes to throw three switches!

Milo A. Jordan, a Commander in the Coast Guard, when I located him in 1973, then on duty in New Orleans, Louisiana, had been a Coast Guard enlisted man standing watch that night on "Cape D." Jordan wrote to me:

> It was during this period when the Duty Officer at Fort Canby [not Capt. Harris at Battery Gunther who was not on duty] alerted his searchlight groups advising that unidentified objects were offshore. Tensions ran high, and in an effort to be 'first on the line' a sergeant ordered 'Turn it on! Let's go!' – and the light came on. An Army officer [barked] an order via field telephone, 'Turn that G D light out or I'll shoot it out.'

Meanwhile, back on Fire Control Hill at "H" Station, Tech. Sergeant Greig and Sergeant Mather jumped out of their bunks in their shorts and dashed up the stairs to the command post in time to hear Corporal "Tully" squawking into a field telephone trying

CAPE DISAPPOINTMENT LIGHTHOUSE
Location: 46°17'N 124°3'W
Nearest town: Ilwaco
Built: 1856
Type: White conical tower
Height above water: 220ft
Height above ground: 53ft
Light source: I electric
 incandescent bulb
Beam: White and Red
Optics: 4th Order
Power: 58,000cp white
 17,000cp red
Seen: 19 miles white
 21 miles red

NOTE: Classic data is from *Light List* 1934.
U.S. Dept. of Commerce, Lighthouse Service
and reflects details then in effect.

The lighthouse at Cape Disappointment is the first primary navigation aid established in the Pacific Northwest and survives to the present time as an honored symbol of history. Locally, it's just called "Cape D." To seaward, the lighthouse sits atop a precipitous cliff 220 feet above the water. Our older undated picture shows the lighthouse probably as it appeared during World War II.

*The complete story of "Cape D" lighthouse is in *Oregon Seacoast Lighthouses* by Jim Gibbs. See bibliography

Base end station for Battery Pratt as it appeared during the war and today its remains, as part of the Military Historical Area of Fort Stevens State Park.

to convince a major at HECP that they were being fired on. Greig told me:

It's probably the only time that a Corporal cussed out a Major and got away with it. Although we had people on duty it appears nobody saw the submarine until they spotted the flash and heard the explosion of the first shell. In our plotting room we had a large, lighted, glass-top table. Under the glass was a map of the Columbia River entrance and all the shores around the river. The RADAR up on North Head told us where the submarine was, but according to our plotting board, the gun flashes were never within range of our guns. The original tracking was by gun flashes computed by triangulation methods from various observation stations. This data was plotted on our operations board mostly from data originating in the Harbor Entrance Control Post. Since the sub plots continued to come in to our board for some time after the firing stopped, it could have been more <u>assumption</u> on our part than fact that the plots we were receiving were from RADAR sources. The flashes of the gun shots were all southwest of our Command Post. They were between us and Tillamook Rock.

At the Battery Russell's command station on top of the parapet, Captain Wood bent over the rangefinder in order to start taking readings. Later Wood told me:

Getting the range with a DPF [Depression-Position Finder] is pretty rough with just gun flashes to sight on. When the sub's guns would fire out there, I'd crank the dog-gone thing and try to get the cross hair on the flash and try to read the range from them. But, by golly, the range drum went clear off the scale, which indicated to me that the range was probably 18 to 20 thousand yards. Our old guns at Battery Russell were good for only 16,000 yards with armor-piercing ammo and only a little bit more with high explosive shells.

The guns at Battery Russell had been sitting out in the Oregon coast weather since 1904 with only a plug in the muzzle and a canvas cover over the breech for protection. When Captain Wood was asked if this long exposure would have affected their range and accuracy, he roared:

No! That wouldn't make any difference. I had the boys load the guns with armor-piercing shells and trip them into battery. I had both guns ready to fire. Hanson, gunpointer on No. 1 gun, was trying to pick up the flashes on his gunsight. I thought if worst came to worst, I'd just fire the guns like field pieces. Zero in on the flashes and start firing over and short as the Field Artillery does. But the sub was down-range from our guns. If we'd been able to get a definite location on him he still would have been beyond our range.

I don't think the sub skipper had any idea he was shelling Battery Russell. He was just dropping a string of shots across the place. It was just an accident that he came close to us. We just happened to be there. *

I asked for clearance to fire. I asked the Field-Officer-of-the-Day up on Fire Control Hill if I could have the searchlights turned on. We had searchlight units all along the beach – one only about 300 yards away. They could have picked up anything out there without any trouble.

The searchlight units had arc lamps noted for their brilliance and ability to split the night with a terrifying splash of blue-white light. At least one of the searchlight crews was as eager as

---

* Jack Wood's speculation turned out to be precisely right but this was not learned until an interview, much later, in Japan, with the sub's commander, Meiji Tagami.

Captain Wood to get the lights into action. At McKenzie Head, Richard Ebi and his card-playing crew members heard the first shot and immediately got busy. In just a couple of minutes they had their generator going thus their light was ready. Private Campbell telephoned the Harbor Entrance Control Post and asked permission to turn the light on the submarine. Captain Wood called from Battery Russell about the same time requesting permission to fire on the sub. They were told that such permission would have to come from Colonel Doney, the Commanding Officer of the Columbia River Defenses.

Where Was Colonel Doney?

Where was the Colonel?

Ebi says that from his high vantage point on McKenzie Head, he watched the submarine <u>seem to travel</u> in a northerly direction across the track of the setting moon, firing as she went. He distinctly heard 14 rounds fired. He knew that his light "could reach a phenomenal distance" and that he could have easily illuminated the submarine so the gun batteries could have seen it. But permission to flip the switch did not come and the unique moment of opportunity was slipping by.

Where was Colonel Doney?

In Battery Clark at Fort Stevens, Captain Platt Davis had four 12-inch mortars ready.

He told the author:

My, did we ever want to fire! The men were so excited about this chance to put our weapons into action and so disappointed at not being permitted to use them that twenty-two of them went over the hill that night. Letting them pull the trigger just once against an enemy target would have been like having a boil lanced. It would have released tension and anxiety even if they didn't hit anything.

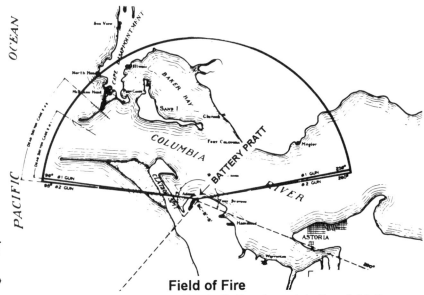

Field of Fire

Battery Pratt (TOP) was the "Ready Battery" on duty the night the Japanese Navy shot at Fort Stevens from the vessel's position at sea. Battery Pratt's firing field might have been effective if the attacker had cruised up the Columbia River, which it did not. The 12-inch Mortar Battery Clark (LOWER) had a circular Field of Fire. Clark's mortars were on the border of effective range.

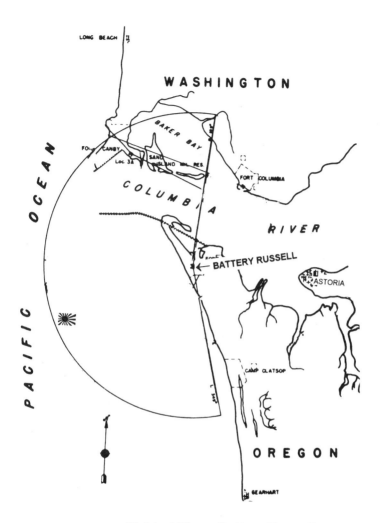

Field of Fire – Battery Russell

The attacking Japanese vessel, Imperial submarine *I-25,* was within the battery's range. This permanent shore battery of 10-inch Disappearing Rifles, did not fire back because no firing order ever came. "We blew it for our Corps," declared an officer after things quieted down. There was a chance to return the enemy's fire, but ... nothing happened.

The San Francisco News

FINAL

Complete N.Y. Stocks

PRICE FIVE CENTS

SAN FRANCISCO, MONDAY, JUNE 22, 1942

ORE. COAST SHELLED!

2nd Alaska Landing

Japanese sub like that 331 feet long, capable of 15,000 miles without refueling, presumed to be one that shelled Vancouver Island, then coast near Astoria, Ore. Arrow points to 4.7-inch gun.

RAIDER HUNTED

TARGETS

COLOR MAP

A map of Alaska to ship and save, showing where Japanese incidents and strategic importance.

(SEE PAGE 8.)

Sub Fires 6 to 9 Times at Beach Near Mouth of Columbia River in 2nd Attack

BLAST ENEMY AT KISKA ISLE

AXIS MEN CONVOY

In San Francisco, the *News*, an afternoon paper, ran this WAR EXTRA by midafternoon on Monday following the Sunday night attack. But in Portland, the *Oregonian* didn't hit the streets until Tuesday morning (see page ii). The *News* used the only photo of a Japanese sub it had, the *I-3* with 4.7-inch gun. This was not the right vessel as *I-25* had an aircraft hangar on foredeck and its gun was 5.5 cm. The picture was effective and no one knew the difference anyway.

What Happened?

The next day, June 22, 1942, a great clamor arose from both military and civilian authorities and from the press to find out exactly what had happened. As might be expected, in a time of surprise and confusion, ear-witnesses to the shelling had many estimates of the number of rounds fired. Captain Wood thought that there were "around a dozen." When his wife heard the first shot, she thought the President had died and it was the beginning of a 21-gun salute, but not that many were fired. She said there were more than "nine" – the number painted on a sign at the entrance to Battery Russell, a few days later.

*   *   *

It occurs that in the Imperial Japanese Navy, many officers as well as enlisted men kept diaries, and there was also the ship's log. From all these sources I have learned there were seventeen shots fired that night. This is the number given by Mr. Fujita and by members of the gun crew who were on deck with Commander Tagami.

Satisfaction

Some of the gunners expressed satisfaction to me at the Tokyo reunion in 1975, about having been at last allowed to "shoot on America," these men having been denied to fire on an earlier mission in December 1941 when their firing orders were canceled at the last minute.

Some of the 17 rounds, of course, may have been duds. Some burst and left craters in the beach or among the skunk cabbages in the marsh behind Battery Russell. Some which may not have ex-

ploded may still be buried in swamp or sand with houses built on them now, over 50 years later!

One shell, the closest one to Battery Russell, smashed the backstop of the baseball diamond. This was about 70 or 80 yards in front of the big guns. Captain Wood says a jagged, circular plate from the base or butt of a shell, and a fragment from the nose of the shell were recovered. Other fragments were found in the camouflage net that covered Battery Russell

> **Editor's Note:**
> In looking toward the sea from the top of Battery Russell in Fort Stevens State Park today, readers are alerted to realize that in the decades since this incident, beach accretion has occurred and all the vegetation is 50-years thicker and higher. In other words, what one sees today, is not at all what the scene looked like in summer 1942.

When Mr. and Mrs. Hitchman returned to their home three miles south of the post after the shelling, they found their sons and daughter huddled together in one bed for mutual security.

Daughter Ardith (now Mrs. Wayne Severson), told me that they had been frightened by an explosion and she had bribed her

Continued on page 70

Arrow (TOP) indicates shell impact site near Hitchman farm house on DeLaura Beach Road. Flying shell missed the house by about 12 yards. See page 60 for impact site. The next morning, Captain Wood extracted this example (LOWER) of shell fragment from the camouflage net that covered Battery Russell.

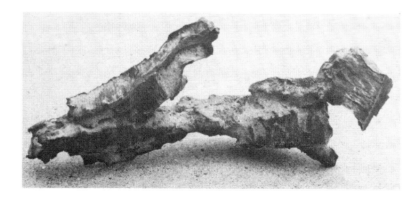

Shell Impact Site on DeLaura Beach Road. The shell shown is gift from U. S. Navy for use in this monument. It is a 5.5-inch where the Japanese 14cm shell is very slightly different. The tree beyond the impact site shows split from being severely damaged when a young sapling. This picture was made in 1973. Twenty years later, the area is heavily overgrown. Many dozens of odd-size fragments (LOWER) were picked up in following weeks.

The DeLaura Beach Road impact site of Japanese
5.5cm shell fired by Imperial Submarine *I-25*.

Colonel Carl S. Doney, Commanding Officer of the Harbor Defenses of the Columbia, appropriately dressed in leggings, steel helmet, gas mask and swagger stick (in left hand) posed for *Oregonian* photographer, the day after the attack, as he showed a shell fragment to local children.

Fragments came in assorted sizes. These pieces from the end plate of the shell.

HISTORICAL LANDMARK

ON JUNE 21, 1942 A 5.5" SHELL EXPLODED HERE. ONE OF 17 FIRED AT COLUMBIA RIVER HARBOR DEFENSE INSTALLATIONS BY THE JAPANESE SUBMARINE I-25. THE ONLY HOSTILE SHELLING OF A MILITARY BASE ON THE U.S. MAINLAND DURING WORLD WAR II AND THE FIRST SINCE THE WAR OF 1812.

Scale model of I-25 on granite monument on DeLaura Beach Road. It was made at Dick Thompson's Astoria Granite Works from blue-prints supplied by Mitsubishi Heavy Industries, Tokyo.

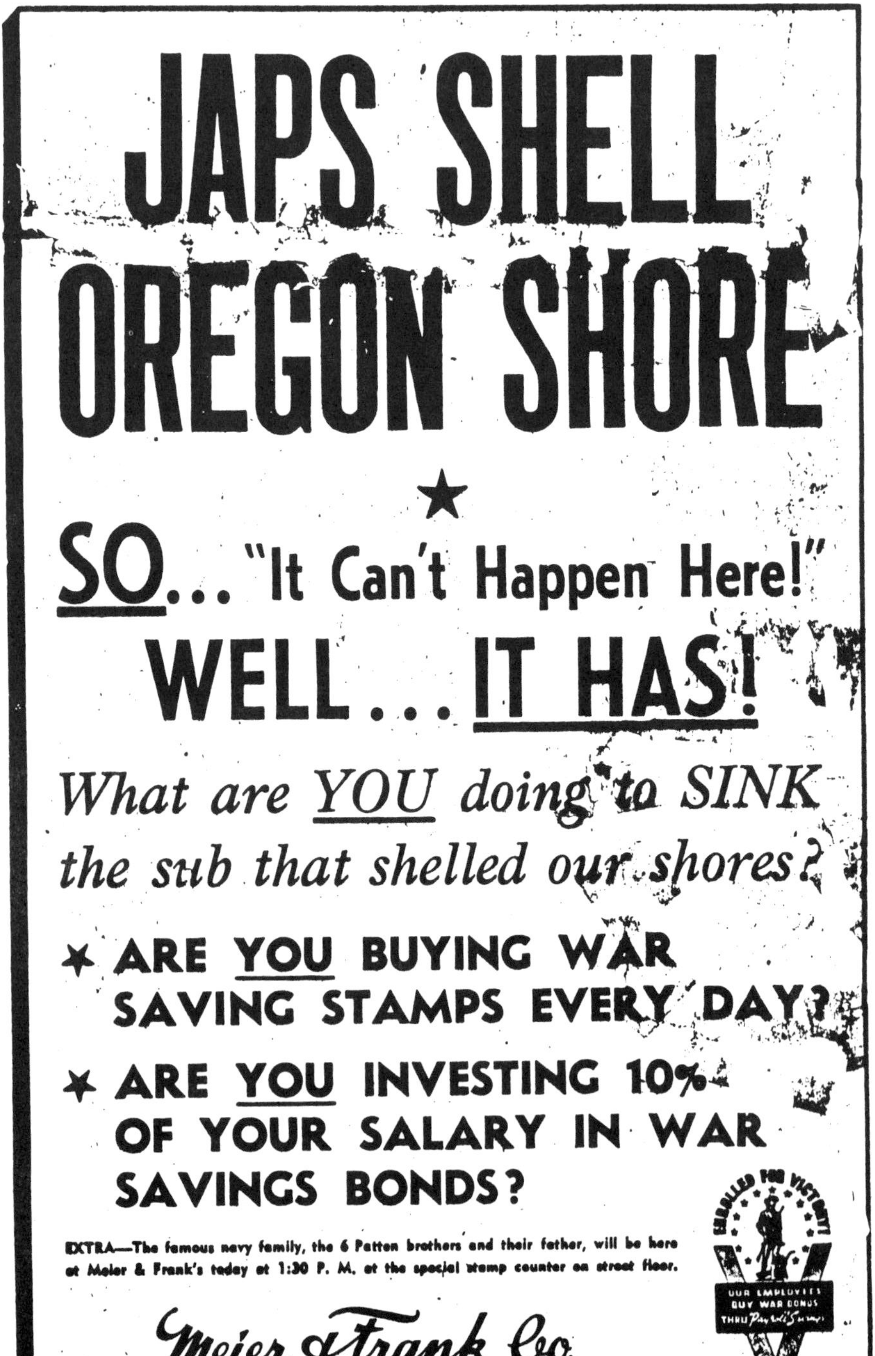

Advertisement from *Oregonian* June 23, 1942

Soldier points to shell fragment (TOP) deeply imbedded in tree after someone with an ax had "gone after it." Fragments of various sizes (LOWER) were found over a wide area.

65

Exploring party of Staff Officers scavenge for souveniers of the attack. They found plenty but a one officer got a little soiled in the process while digging in mud hole. Colonel Carl S. Doney, with swagger stick (arrow) is second from left.

Oregonian photographer waited for "diving officer" to roll his left sleeve down before he snapped this picture. Colonel Doney, now with swagger stick in left hand (arrow), reaches for the shell fragment.

Coast in Panic, Jap Radio Blares

TOKYO, June 23 (Japanese broadcast recorded by UP, San Francisco)—Tokyo radio said Tuesday that as a result of the shelling of the Oregon coast late Sunday night, residents of the United States from Canada to Mexico "are panic stricken and are leaving in huge numbers for the interior."

67

The pond among the skunk cabbages (TOP), where a shell, or at least fragments from one, landed, was a popular place to be to have one's picture made. Men from 249th Coast Artillery (LOWER) pose in shell hole on the beach. Man at left holds something in his right hand. Fragment?

Officers (Colonel Doney, center) scan out to sea in direction from where submarine *I-25* shelled the night before. All of this vegetation is considerably higher 50 years later.

69

Continued from page 58

brothers by offering them 25 cents of her potato-hoeing money if she could snuggle in bed with them until their parents came home.

Army investigators next morning found remains of an exploded shell along DeLaura Beach Road 125 yards inland from the Hitchman house. The shell's trajectory apparently had been parallel with the road and only about *12 yards in front of the bedrooms* where the children huddled. It had hissed over an ammunition dump just inside the north fence of Camp Clatsop. When it exploded it shattered a tree and blasted a big hole in the edge of the swamp.

One fragment from this shell caused damage that was not discovered until 16 months later. A power outage caused maintenance men of the Pacific Power and Light Company to wonder why a breakdown had occurred in a low-risk area. The break was on DeLaura Beach Road nearly across the road and within sight of the Hitchman farmhouse. Pacific Power linemen found a nick in the wire's copper cladding. This exposed the steel core to the corrosive effects of the salt air. Eventually the steel wire rusted through and broke therefore, the neighborhood lights went out.

Investigators concluded that a fragment from the Japanese shell had done the damage. Pacific Power thus became one of the few stateside American firms to sustain damage on the United States mainland from an enemy attack in World War II.

Fragments of this shell and others that exploded were found in the following weeks by souvenir hunters who tramped through the marshes and along the beach, but the number carried away greatly exceeded the actual number of pieces of Japanese shells. The Hitchman sons and other neighborhood boys made a little money selling broken pieces of cast iron stove lids, fire-pot doors, and other metal from the city dump as "genuine Japanese shrapnel"* to eager tourists.

Rumors of men having been hurt have persisted through the years but none of them have held up under close scrutiny. Further, tales of "dead Japanese that washed ashore and were secretly

---

*Use of the word "shrapnel" has become corrupted to mean any piece of flying fragment from a bomb or artillery shell. But "shrapnel" is actually from a projectile that contains small metal balls or shrapnel rings fused to explode in the air above troops. This projectile was invented by a British artilleryman General Henry Shrapnel in 1784. None of the shells fired against U. S. soil by elements of the Japanese Navy contained "shrapnel."

View toward the ocean (TOP) from Battery Russell base end station in 1974. Same view (LOWER) in 1992. The vegetation has grown therefore visitors today should not expect to see the same view afforded the Coast Artillerymen a half-century ago.

Battery Russell base end station (LEFT) from which pictures on page 71 were made. Square building (LOWER RIGHT) is believed to be former power house for searchlights (SEE INSET).

buried," which is unreported in all of the submarines' logs, all add to the folklore.

Observers who claim to have "seen" submarine *I-25* have it going in various directions. Some claim is was headed south. Others say it was going north. One man from a high vantage point says he saw it sailing "in a wide arc, firing as she went." If some reports are to be believed, it had made a 360° turn before retiring. Talks of how long the submarine stayed and how it maneuvered are undoubtedly exaggerated over time and with frequent retelling. Many people saw the muzzle flashes, some even as far away as on a hill in the city of Astoria. It is doubtful that anyone saw the submarine's long, black hull quite some distance at sea running no lights, and only emitting gun flashes.

Battery Russell base end station. Tillamook Head in background. Tillamook Rock Lighthouse (arrow) is 1-mile off shore. Some claim the submarine came alongside, but the *I-25*'s *log* does not reveal this.

Manana

Out in the bay a bit north of "White Evelyn," the Coast Guard's converted yacht *Manana II* had been drifting toward the south shore inside the bar. The skipper, Chief Motor Machinist's Mate George W. Cooper, had barely gotten into his bunk when his boson's mate called, "Mr. Cooper, Fort Stevens is shooting at us!"

Cooper, who lived in Grants Pass when interviewed, told me:

I was on the deck in a second. All was quiet on shore when suddenly from the sea I saw a flash and a few seconds later heard a "*whupp*." The outline of a conning tower was seen in the flash; then all was dark again. A submarine was firing on Fort Stevens!

I raced to the radio room and called Coast Guard radio at Grays Harbor in clear language—no time for messing with any code. I said, 'Submarine bearing south west, distance 2-3 miles south of south jetty, firing at Fort Stevens.'

As far as I have been able to learn, this radio report was the first news of the attack flashed to anyone.

By this time our crews were alerted by the shooting. We didn't have to sound Battle Stations.

William Gaither, commanding the *USCGC 402*, put his ship alongside the *Manana* and we talked to each other from about ten feet. His armament was greater than mine. He had a Lewis .30-caliber air-cooled machine gun and a 37-mm gun mounted on the deck. Gaither asked, 'Do you think I ought to ram the sub?' I said, 'No, because our [wooden] ships will never survive the ramming against the steel hull of the submarine.'

The Lightship *Relief* was on the Columbia River Lightship station the night the Japanese Navy shelled the Oregon coast. This picture was made in Lake Washington where the relic serves as a floating museum.

The Lightship

When the sub left about midnight, it ran on the surface to the west passing several fishing boats and the blacked-out lightship *Relief* on the Columbia River Lightship station.

The lightship's log indicates that flashes were seen ten miles south-southeast at 11:45 p.m., but does not identify the sources of the flashes. Ben. J. Norman, Seattle, a Coast Guard fireman on the coal-burning *Relief,* was on the bridge when he saw the flashes. He told me:

> The beacon light on the lightship was off and the ship was blacked out except for our very small anchor light. We were unarmed. If the *Relief* had been attacked, all I could have done was to throw coal at them!

Commander Tagami told me he did not see the blacked-out lightship but even if he had seen it, he probably would have ignored it. Mr. Hasegawa, commander of the *I-25's* sister, the *I-26,* wrote to me:.

Japanese submariners were trained to attack big-sized targets such as the major battleships or aircraft carriers. In many cases torpedoes shot at shallow-bottom boats were apt to jump out of the surface like, say a dolphin, and be wasted without any result. Captain Tagami, my class-mate, said he did not see the Columbia River lightship. Therefore he has no memory of approaching it.

News of the Fort Stevens attack made the front page of the *New York Times,* June 23, 1942:

FOE'S SHELLS FALL ON OREGON COAST

Reporting in the *New York Times* on June 28, 1942, Richard L. Neuberger wrote:

It was the first personal taste of war for residents of the Oregon Coast, who, contrary to Tokyo's imaginative version of the incident, watched and listened to the 'show' and kept their heads, no matter how much their hearts might have been thumping.

Shell cart with six-inch shells on exhibit in Fort Stevens Historical Museum.

WHY DIDN'T WE SHOOT BACK WHEN THE JAPS SHELLED OREGON?

TODAY'S JOURNAL

The *Oregon Journal* did a front page feature story about the American Legion's annual convention in Medford (June 23, 1972 the 30th anniversary of the Japanese attack) and provided an in-depth feature article by Bert Webber about the event. (See bibliography)

The Decision About a "Messy Inconvenience"

For more than five decades, there have been rumors, speculation, myth, and just plain lies about why the defenses of the Columbia did not strike back when fired on by the Japanese Navy.

Captain Wood, at Battery Russell, was an experienced Coast Artillery officer. But he said it was dark, he could not see the vessel except for momentary, dull reflection of the flash on the sub's newly painted black hull. Nevertheless, he estimated that the flashes came from a distance of 18,000 to 20,000 yards. He told me this was a "pure guess." He knew his guns were good for about 16,000 yards with the armor-piercing shells with which they were loaded. Even though he was apparently beyond range, that is not the reason he did not fire. He asked for searchlight support and permission to fire, but authorization never came. Captain Harris at Fort Canby also wanted to fire, but no one would give him permission.

Bennett Loftsgaard, who saw the flashes from near the south jetty, declared, "We were closer to the submarine than anyone else and we couldn't <u>see</u> it."

Sergeant Ernest Fieguth said:

I could see the gun flashes, but our old 75's wouldn't shoot that far, but we were sure in the front row to view the action.

The specifications for 10-inch guns like those at Battery Russell give the maximum range as 16,200 yards. The men who were using these particular guns estimated the guns' range from 14,000 to 16,000 yards.

Regardless, whether the submarine was within range, those in authority believed that it was not, therefore made the decision not to fire.

An arsenal of weapons – machine guns, French 75's, mortars, and heavy coast artillery guns were manned. Searchlight crews were at the ready. But no one gave an order to pull a trigger or pressed a button to activate the carefully prepared systems.

What was the reasoning behind the decision not to fire? Replies to inquiries came from many places – Hong Kong, Ottawa, Florida, Victoria, South Carolina, Virginia – but the probable answer came from Saipan in the Mariana Islands. In a letter written on Christmas Day 1972, former Major Robert M. Huston wrote:

I was the Senior Duty Officer on duty at the Group Fire Control Station at Fire Control Hill the night that the Japanese submarine fired on the beach area. As Senior Duty Officer, I represented Colonel Kenneth Rounder, the Group Commander. I asked all stations to report the range of the flashes ... we determined that the submarine was about 2,000 to 3,000 yards out of range of the nearest battery – Battery Russell. Captain Wood requested permission to open fire. I refused permission on the basis:

78

1. The submarine was not in range and was very likely firing a reconnaissance mission to spot location of our batteries.

2. The submarine outranged us by about 4,000 yards, being a modern 5-inch (approximately) gun on a barbette carriage. Our old disappearing guns were limited in range. Due to the disappearing carriage they could only be elevated a little over 14°. Battery Russell had a maximum range of about 14,000 yards, having been designed for use against 1900 vintage cruisers and battleships.

3. We had no RADAR at that time and we had to depend on visual observation of the flashes, or use searchlights, which certainly wasn't advisable when you are outranged and the target is out of range.

Jack Wood wanted very much to open fire. I made a decision [not to fire] which I thought was tactically sound and later supported (I was told) by the Commanding General, 9th Coast Artillery District in San Francisco. I wish I could have gone along with Jack became of the effect on morale.

This is the official answer. These are the men who made the decisions which are clear enough and logical enough once one knows the basis for them. Zed Harris, a long-time loyal member of the Coast Artillery Corps, has his own opinion of the major result of the events of June 21, 1942.

Captain Zed Harris:
The death blow to the Harbor Defense units was dealt the night of the Japanese attack on Fort Stevens. There was no return fire. Whether the fire would have hit anything or not wasn't the point. With hundreds of guns and mortars along both Atlantic and Pacific shores, and thousands of men at the ready, we *blew it* for our Corps when we had a chance to shoot – and didn't.

Where was Colonel Carl S. Doney, the Commanding Officer of the Columbia River Defenses during all of this excitement?

I made a special trip to San Francisco, when I learned he was living there in retirement, to keep an appointment we had made by telephone. We had a cordial but business-like meeting. But the elderly colonel did not really seem interested in talking with me about this matter. I asked Col. Doney where he was that night in 1942? Sitting in his small apartment on Clement Street, he related to me:

I was in bed in my quarters where all good post commanders should be near midnight on a Sunday night. I had competent duty officers and they were keeping the store. The whole affair was a messy inconvenience. I got the

**Colonel Carl S. Doney,
USA (Ret.)**
—Bert Webber photo

phone call just after I heard big guns, so I got up, dressed, called for my driver then I went to the Command Post [in the HECP building].

I asked Col. Doney what he had to say about the range of the target from any of the big guns at the closest forts – Stevens and Canby. He seemed not to want to talk about that. After a long silence, during which I kept biting at my lip telling myself to keep still, he'll eventually speak, the long-retired and now ill colonel, striving to avoid eye contact and definitely appearing uncomfortable seeming to feel as if he had been put in a West Point Military Academy "brace," gazed out through the small window of his basement apartment. From his worn, overstuffed chair he suddenly declared:

They were out of our range and there was no reason to fire – give our position away. We had them tracked all the time and they were from 500 to 1,000 yards out of our maximum range. A big flash from shore would have given them a pinpoint and been absolutely useless.

By the time Colonel Doney arrived at the HECP, the enemy naval vessel had gone.

Without having consulted his superior officer, Maj. General Robert H. Lewis, at Fort Lewis, Washington, Colonel Doney, as Commander of the Columbia River Defenses was the spokesman and right or not, validated the decisions of his duty officers not to use the searchlights and not to return the fire.

80

How the Japanese Did It

Very solid evidence has been received from Japan that negates all the claims, and official statements, that submarine *I-25* was <u>beyond</u> the range of Battery Russell's 10-inch guns at Fort Stevens.

This part of the research required close concentration and stamina due to the various trips, such as the visit with Colonel Doney, and others on the American side, and many round-trip letters between the author and former military men in Japan, with additional work on each end for translations.

I sent Commander Tagami a photocopy of a 1935 British Chart with Japanese overprinting showing a penciled-in track "alleged course of Japanese submarine to Fort Stevens area in 1942."

Tagami immediately replied. He wrote excellent English and used a typewriter. He declared it was *"Not my chart!"* He said that he was using a "very, very old chart printed in U.S.A." that has not been preserved. In his letter in February 1974, he sketched the river entrance from memory and marked "fortifications" on the <u>north side</u> of the Columbia River. Then he drew in the location of a "destroyer and submarine base" at Tongue Point, about 15 miles upriver. In an interview with a newsman in 1950, Tagami said he was firing in the direction of the submarine base.

Although the naval station at Tongue Point was never equipped to service submarines, and over the years only a few submarines ever docked there, its development into a submarine base was contemplated at one time. A 1918 revision of an 1898 navigation chart indicates Tongue Point as a "Proposed Submarine Base." Commander Tagami had every reason to believe he was shooting in the direction of a submarine base.

Also on the old chart are notations showing a row of heavy guns atop Cape Disappointment. These are obviously the "fortifications" Tagami was referring to. Thus, he placed his submarine

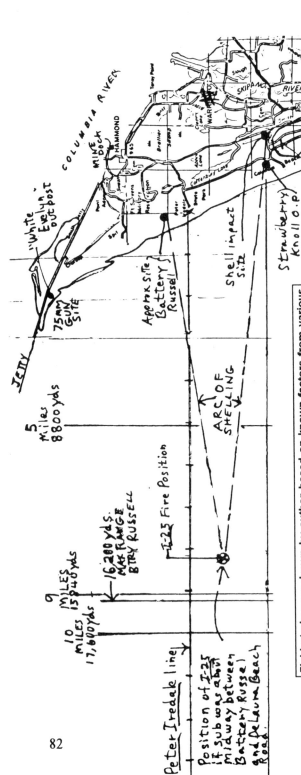

Field study map drawn by author based on known factors from various resources. This map was presented to Captain Meiji Tagami during the reunion/reception in Tokyo in 1975. With interpreter, Tagami, who read English but did not speak it, agreed with all items relative to his ship, Imperial Navy submarine *I-25*. On studying this chart, this retired sea captain shook his head and declared, "To risk my ship and my crew with such foolishness [as to be under those big guns] was unthinkable."

JETTY

"White Evelyn" outpost

COLUMBIA RIVER

MINE DOCK

HAMMOND

SKIPANON RIVER

WARR

CAMP CLATSOP

Locked gate

Strawberry Knoll O.P.

Shell impact site

Approx. Site Battery Russell

75MM GUN SITE

5 Miles 8800 yds

ARC OF SHELLING

I-25 Fire Position

16,200 yds. Max Range Btry Russell

9 Miles 15,840 yds

10 Miles 17,600 yds

Peter Iredale line

Position of I-25 (sub was about midway between Battery Russell and Delaura Beach Road)

82

Tokyo Reception July 31, 1975 at Navy Club for Bert and Margie Webber and Reunion of *I-25* and *I-26* Veterans

Veterans concerned with the Fort Stevens Attack who provided private diaries, photographs and recollections about the action off the Oregon Coast June 21, 1942: (14) Sonar operator and artist Kou Maki, (15) Aircraft pilot and deck officer Nobuo Fujita, (16) Executive Officer Tatsuo Tsukuduo, (17) Torpedoman Shoji Aizawa, (18) Gunner Sadao Iijima, (20) Engineman Togoro Okamoto, (21) *I-25* Commander Meiji Tagami, (27) Gunner Sensuke Tao. Bert and Margie Webber are (7, 10). Minoru (Yokota) Hasagawa (19) *I-26* skipper.

83

south of the river, presumably out of range of Cape Disappoint-ment's guns. I have a copy of that chart. Tagami's recollections were correct!

Following my request of Admiral James S. Russell, (U.S.N. retired) for assistance, he wrote to his friend Admiral Hiroichi Samejima* asking Admiral Samejima if he might make inquiries in Japan about Meiji Tagami's attack at Fort Stevens. In reply, Admiral Samejima says that Commander Tagami positioned *I-25* at "13,000 yards range approaching the limit from the viewpoint of escape from attack by [an] enemy vessel." Cdr. Tagami told me he was at the "10-fathom curve," on his chart, which was barely minimum depth if he had to dive.

Tatsuo Tsukuduo, former executive officer on *I-25*, describes the 14-cm (5.5-inch) deck gun as being a 1922 model with a maximum range of 14,000 meters (15,310 yards).

Another crew member, Sadao Iijima, a gunner who did some of the firing, wrote to me confirming the fact that the naval gun had a range of 14,000 meters but that he fired from 10,000 meters (*10,936 yards*) from shore – *just over 6 miles* – (recalling that Battery Russell's maximum range was 9 miles). Iijima also said the gun was a 1922 design which had been manufactured in 1936.

Sensuke Tao, who also fired some of the shells, told me that when he fired, the gun was set "dead center-zero degrees, firing range 10,000 meters."**

If these men who were on the submarine and took active part in the attack are to be credited, *I-25* was *unquestionably within range of Fort Stevens' guns* when it hurled shells. One landed on the baseball diamond in front of Battery Russell demolishing the backstop. Another landed nearly one mile inland on the DeLaura Beach Road.

Because of the wide discrepancy in reports of the "firing run" – in what direction was the submarine traveling while shooting – Admiral Samejima also inquired into that. He wrote to me:

---

* Admiral Samejima was the chief official of the Japanese Maritime Self Defense Force (Navy). Later, when I visited with him in his office in Tokyo, we continued the discussion.

** The friendly chat, Mr. Tsukuduo interpreting, with these former submariner's, was during the reception for me and Mrs. Webber, and reunion of the Imperial Japanese Navy submarine crews (*I-25* and *I-26*) at the Navy Club in Tokyo on July 31, 1975.

Key People

Meiji Tagami.
(left) **As Commander of *I-25***
(right) **As civilian mid-1970's**

(TOP ROW) **Kou Maki, sonarman, artist; Togoro Okamoto, electric engineman; Sadao Iijima, gunner.** (LOWER ROW) **Tatsuo Tsukuduo, *I-25* Executive Officer; Shoji Aizawa, torpedoman; Sensuke Tao, gunner.**

Tsukuduo, later Admiral, became Sup't of new Naval Academy, is presently Chief Priest of the Navy Shrine.

There is no track chart of *I-25* showing her firing runs on June 21, 1942 while shelling the fort at the entrance to the Columbia River. *I-25* did the firing with stern facing the beach and with deck gun centered shooting over the stern.

The only movement of the vessel during the attack was natural drift of the offshore current. In short, *I-25 was standing still!* The engineers kept the diesels running and as one of them told me in jocular form, "– was just like having foot on clutch ready to 'dig out' fast if we had been attacked."

As has been mentioned, at the finish of the firing, Commander Tagami ordered everyone off the deck except for two lookouts. Then he headed west past the Columbia River Lightship. His track from the area of the Columbia River was due west to about 46°N. - 164° 05'W. arriving at that point on June 27 (Japan time). From this position off Dutch Harbor, he sailed *I-25* back to Japan. □

The only pair of 10-in guns of Disappearing Carriages located after a world-wide search, were in the Philippine Islands. Although there were some efforts to obtain the guns to be installed in Battery Russell at Fort Stevens, a delegation from the State of Washington had a prior request. The guns were moved to Whidby Island and can be seen today in Fort Casey State Park. Shown here is one of the guns "in Battery."

Commander Tagami's Realization of His Dangerous Decision

When Meiji Tagami, the *I-25* skipper, had his men bring the submarine to a stop at a specific place in the Pacific Ocean, off the Oregon Coast, he felt quite secure with his endeavor. Submarines sit low in the water. He believed any coast watchers along the Oregon shore would be unable to see his ship because his vessel had been painted black. He showed no running lights. Also, he was several miles at sea.

Tagami acknowledged through an interpreter (Admiral Tatsuo Tsukuduo, his former Executive Officer on *I-25*), when Tagami, Tsukuduo and Webber were together at the 1975 reception in Tokyo:

"Somehow I feel more than lucky to be here tonight. I had no idea there were such big cannon right in front of me. With expert [gun] crews I believe *I-25* would have been sunk easily in only a few shots. When you wrote to me and sent pictures of the Battery [Russell] and those great mortars [Gunther and Clark] I was sick with fright for the damage they could have done to my *I-25.*

"If I had any idea those cannons were right in front of me I would never have been there!

"To risk my ship and my crew [108 men on this mission] with such foolishness [being immediately in front of the guns] was unthinkable."

—Meiji Tagami to Bert Webber, Tokyo, July 31, 1975

—Meiji Tagami died in 1981

Kou Maki's sketch of *I-25* with his signature of authencity. The drawing was presented to Bert Webber at the reception in Tokyo. After the war, Maki spent his life as a baker.

Persons who have read the master book, *Silent Siege*, know that the aircraft shown on deck was a collapsable (Erector Set) airplane. Its wings and pontoons came off for stowing in the hangar which is the elongation of the conning tower. Compressed air was used to launch the plane from its rails on foredeck. On return to the submarine, the plane landed on the sea then, with a derrick, was hoisted aboard. Set up time was about 45 minutes. The knockdown about 30 minutes. Pilot Fujita, who was on all three voyages of *I-25* to northwest coast of the United States, has returned a number of times for visits in recent years.

Former Pilot Fujita, 85, died of lung cancer at his home in Tsuchiura City, Japan on October 1, 1997 (Japan date).

Flight Officer
Nubuo Fujita

Battery Russell today

Reunion at Fort Stevens

Veterans assemble for special program sponsored by Friends of Old Fort Stevens (FOOFS) on June 21, 1992 at Battery Russell. (top - left to right) **Vernon Greig, Vardel Nelson, Donald Moy.** Some of the fellows were not quite as spry as they were half-a-century earlier.

Recalling that the commanders at Fort Stevens would not allow Battery Russell to return the fire of the Japanese in 1942, by arrangement with the Oregon Army National Guard, a 3-inch gun on top of the parapet, returned the fire even though it was 50 years later. The crowd, in the hundreds, cheered.

60-inch WW-II model searchlight on permanent exhibit in the Military Historical Area at Fort Stevens State park.

91

Bibliography

Baker, Lillian. *American and Japanese Relocation in World War-II, Fact, Fiction & Fallacy.* Webb Research Group. 1990.

Gibbs, James A. *Oregon Seacoast Lighthouses.* Webb Research Group. 1992.

Hanft, Marshall. "Fort Stevens, A Trace of Nostalgia" in *Northwest Magazine (Oregonian).* Apr. 28. 1968.

_____. *Fort Stevens, Oregon's Defender at the River of the West.* Oregon State Printer. 1980.

Kirchner, D. P. and Emanuel R. Lewis. "American Harbor Defenses: The Final Era" in *Proceedings.* U.S. Naval Inst. 1970. pp. 95-98.

Lewis, Emanuel Raymond. *Seacoast Fortifications of the United States.* Smithsonian. 1970.

Maki, Kou. *The Mission of I-25; Secret Document on American Mainland Attack* (in Japanese). Ushio (Tokyo). 1956. Based on Kou's diary when he was known as Kou Okamura and was Chief Petty Officer in *I-25.* Republished with pencil sketches 1962.

Neuberger, Richard L. and Lawrence E. Davis. "Enemy Off Shore Stirs West Coast" in *New York Times* June 28, 1942, Sec 4, p.6.

Edwards, Herman. "Fort Stevens Target of Jap Submarine's Guns; 9 Shells Scream Ashore On Oregon Coast - Army Announces Damage Nil" in *Oregonian.* June 23, 1942. p. 1.

Page, Robert M. *The Origin of Radar.* Anchor. 1962.

Senchio Sosho (Boeicho Kenshujo Senshishitsu) The Aleutian's. (Vol. 29) Japan Defense Agency, War History Section. Tokyo. n.d. [*ca.* 1974].

Watts, Anthony J. and Brian C. Gordon. *The Imperial Japanese Navy.* Doubleday. 1971.

Webber, Bert. *Retaliation: Japanese Attacks and Allied Countermeasures on the Pacific Coast in World War II.* Oregon State Univ. Press. 1975.

_____. *Silent Siege-III, Japanese Attacks on North America in World War-II, Ships Sunk, Air Raids, Bombs Dropped, Civilians Killed – Documentary.* Webb Research Group. 1992.

_____. "U. S. Guns Were Ready! Why Didn't They Fire Back at Japanese Sub Shelling Oregon Coast?" in *Oregon Journal.* June 23, 1972 [1-DOT EDITION].

Webber on Rota, Mariana Islands, with WW-II Japanese gun.

About the Author

Bert Webber has been creating feature stories for newspapers and magazines, and writing full-length books seemingly forever, for he got his start in George Washington High School in San Francisco. He went into the Regular Army Signal Corps at the Presidio of San Francisco in 1940. He was serving in Alaska, where he learned photography, at the time of Pearl Harbor and was appointed Signal Corps Photographer. Later he was ordered to the Signal Corps Photographic Center (Paramount Studios) in Astoria, New York, where he studied cinematography and emerged as a news-reel cameraman. Along with this new skill, he applied all of his picture-making experiences on assignments in Scotland, England, Belgium as well as two tours in France.

After the war, Webber operated a commercial photographic business then he entered Whitworth College where he graduated in journalism and library science. While a school librarian, he earned the Master of Library Science with studies at Portland State University and the University of Portland.

Webber retired from librarianship in 1970 to devote all of his time to research photojournalism, the result of which has been over fifty books. His prime topics deal with unique subjects in Oregon history, the Oregon Trail and aspects of World War II about which books had not previously been written. He is the acknowledged international authority concerning the Japanese attacks against the mainland of North America during World War II.

He is listed in *Who's Who in the West, Who's Who in America, Contemporary Authors,* and was awarded the "Decree of Merit" in *Men of Achievement,* International Biographical Centre, Cambridge, England.

For fun, Webber plays Euphonium in the Southern Oregon Symphonic Band, where he also serves on the Board of Control. He lives with his wife, Margie, a retired Registered Nurse, in Oregon's Rogue River Valley. They have four children and eight grandchildren. □

Index

Photographs and maps are shown in **bold *italic*** type